BIG PHARMA
AND THE
OPIOID
EPIDEMIC

FROM VICODIN TO HEROIN

by Eric Braun

Consultant:
David Herzberg, Associate Professor of History,
University of Buffalo College of Arts and Sciences

COMPASS POINT BOOKS
a capstone imprint

Informed! is published by Compass Point Books, an imprint of Capstone.
1710 Roe Crest Drive
North Mankato, Minnesota 56003

www.capstonepub.com

Library of Congress Cataloging-in-Publication Data is available on the Library of Congress website.
ISBN: 978-0-7565-6411-7 (library binding)
ISBN: 978-0-7565-6560-2 (paperback)
ISBN: 978-0-7565-6412-4 (ebook PDF)

Summary: More than 130 people a day in the U.S. die from opioid overdoses. Addiction to legal and illegal opioids has been declared a national crisis. What caused this massive problem? Can the crisis be slowed or reversed? Students will get practical tips on how to help someone suffering from an addiction or experiencing an overdose, and learn about how the nation is trying to deal with the crisis.

Image Credits
Alamy: Roy Langstaff, 8, The History Collection, 11 (bottom); Associated Press: South Florida Sun-Sentinel/Carline Jean, 22, Wilson Ring, 51; Dreamstime: Jerry Coli, 27; Getty Images: Boston Globe, 46–47, Kerem Yucel, 25, Spencer Platt, 35, The Washington Post, 20 (bottom); Newscom: BSIP, 29, Reuters/Brian Snyder, 28, Reuters/Joe Skipper, 16, Sipa USA/Kris Tripplaar, 45, TNS/Rich Sugg, 18, TNS/Tiffany Tompkins, 53, ZUMA Press/Cheriss May, 41, ZUMA Press/Octavio Jones, 23, ZUMA Press/Philip Poupin, 33, ZUMA Press/Robin Rayne, 38; Shutterstock: argus, cover (monitor lines), DFree, 42, ed2806, cover (crushed pills), 32, gabriel12, 14, H_Ko, 31, Malik Haris, 12, nevodka, 55, 56, 57, Northfoto, 43, sub job, cover (pills), 4, 11 (top), 20 (top), 34, 40, 54, 61, 63, yusia, 36; Wikimedia: Drug Enforcement Administration, 5

Editorial Credits
Editor: Michelle Bisson; Designer: Brann Garvey; Media Researcher: Eric Gohl; Production Specialist: Kathy McColley

Consultant Credits
David Herzberg, Associate Professor of History, University of Buffalo College of Arts and Sciences

All internet sites appearing in back matter were available and accurate when this book was sent to press.

Printed and bound in the USA.

PA99

TABLE OF CONTENTS

CHAPTER ONE

The **Crisis**

It started out as three friends getting together to have some fun. In November 2018, 19-year-old Gunner Bundrick and two friends went out on a Friday night in their hometown of Prescott Valley, Arizona. Later, they came back to Gunner's family home. They stayed up playing video games and eating pizza. It was a scene you could find in millions of homes on any given night. At some point, best friends Gunner and Jake Morales took a painkiller—perhaps to get high before bed.

But the pills were not what the boys thought they were. Rather, they were laced with a much more powerful opioid. Soon, the two boys were unconscious and making loud, gurgling noises. The third friend thought they were snoring and left. But the boys were not snoring. They were struggling to breathe.

They were dying.

They did everything they could," Jake's mom said later, "but it was too late."

When Gunner's mother found them the next morning, their skin was blue. Hysterical, she called paramedics. But the paramedics were unable to save the boys. "They did everything they could," Jake's mom said later, "but it was too late. The fentanyl was too fast."

Fentanyl is an extremely dangerous drug that can be lethal even in small amounts. It is 50 times more potent than heroin and up to 100 times more potent than morphine. The amount of fentanyl in the pills that killed Gunner and Jake was equal to about three grains of salt.

The amount of fentanyl needed to overdose is even less than the tiny amount shown next to this penny.

Widespread Addiction and Death

That kind of strength is scary to health officials working to fight the effects of opioids in the United States. What makes it even scarier is that it has become so common. In 2017, about 70,000 Americans died of drug overdoses. Most of those were from fentanyl and other opioids. That makes the opioid epidemic the worst health crisis in U.S. history.

The opioid crisis affects people from all walks of life, though it has hit economically depressed communities especially hard. It affects people of every race and every creed. It affects the old and the young.

Fact

Drug overdoses now kill more people every year than died during the deadliest years of previous crises. Annual deaths from car crashes peaked in 1972, when nearly 55,000 died. The HIV/AIDS crisis reached its peak in 1995. That year nearly 51,000 people died.

Opioid addiction and deaths have seeped into every facet of our communities. In Philadelphia, a man injected heroin into his hand on a city bus while passengers watched him (and one recorded him on video). In Cincinnati, a woman overdosed in her baby's room in a children's hospital. People get high, and many have overdosed, in churches, fast-food restaurants, public libraries, public restrooms, parks, under bridges, and in the streets.

And the crisis doesn't only affect users and addicts. Young children, even toddlers, are dying after accidentally ingesting opioids left out by adults. Other kids are left orphaned by parents who overdose. Or they are forced into foster care when their parents go to prison or go away for treatment. Others simply live the dangerous and unpredictable life that comes from having addicted parents. They see their parents stoned or helpless. Sometimes they see them out of control, screaming and crying. Strangers come in and out of their home to buy or use drugs, putting these kids' safety at risk.

To get an idea of just how quickly the deadly crisis is growing, consider the city of Hartford, Connecticut. In just one night in June 2019, five people died of overdoses. That brought the total number of drug deaths for the first half of 2019 in Hartford to 47. That was just a few less than the 51 drug deaths for the whole of the previous year. That same week in June, nine people *almost* died. They were saved with an overdose-reversing drug.

Police in Hartford reported that they are seeing something else that many communities are seeing. More people are overdosing on fentanyl when they think they are taking something else. The drug is getting mixed into other, unregulated drugs. People with opioid addiction may seek out these counterfeit drugs illegally. Suppliers who make the pills often use fentanyl instead of other opioids because it is cheaper and more powerful. But fentanyl is so powerful that even a tiny difference in dosage can change its potency greatly. A small dose of fentanyl can be deadly.

Advertisements now try to alert people to the risks of using fentanyl.

Life Expectancy

The crisis has gotten so bad that Americans' life expectancy has gone down for the first time since World War II. A person born in 2019 is expected to live four months less than a person born just three years ago—a direct result of the opioid crisis.

"The idea that a developed wealthy nation like ours has declining life expectancy just doesn't seem right," said an official at the Centers for Disease Control (CDC). Robert Anderson and his colleagues have been tracking statistics related to the drug crisis. "If you look at the other wealthy countries of the world, they're not seeing the same thing," he said.

How did things get so bad in the United States? How did it start? The answer lies in something we all share, one of the most basic human feelings: pain.

Fostered by Opioids

A young woman wrote in *The New York Times* about her experience living with addicted parents. Lisa Marie Basile wrote that both of her parents had used opioids since she was a little girl. At age eight, her mother locked her "screaming, doped-up" father out of the house. When she was 12, she banged on a locked public bathroom door while her mom got high inside.

Most of all, she remembered a sunny apartment and normal life before the drugs. And then, she wrote, "Addiction poisoned everything."

Her father's addiction first led him to rehab, but he ended up in prison. Lisa spent one Christmas in a homeless shelter with her mom and brother. The next morning, she and her brother walked her mother to a methadone clinic. Neither of her parents had the money or support needed to go into long-term rehab. As a result of the parents' addiction, the state took the kids away to live with a foster family. Though her parents had struggled with addiction, Lisa remembered them fondly. And she considered herself lucky: They hadn't died.

By the time Lisa finished high school, her mom had gotten clean. Lisa moved back in with her for a while, and they rebuilt their relationship. Lisa even reconnected with her dad. Her story is a sad but hopeful one. Addiction is cruel and deadly and indiscriminate. But many people had compassion for her and her family. That is how they all made it through. As she wrote, "I carry that compassion with me each day—it is as vital to me as blood and air, and it colors my entire life."

CHAPTER TWO

The **Pain**

Advances in chemistry in the 1800s helped researchers isolate opioids such as morphine and heroin from the opium poppy. But although opioids are powerful and highly addictive, they were not regulated in the United States. After the Civil War, doctors prescribed them liberally. Often, they were used to relieve the pain of soldiers suffering from battle wounds. Many doctors prescribed opioids not only for severe pain, but also for other health problems, such as diarrhea and toothaches.

Civil War soldiers suffered horribly from battle wounds—and many died. For those who survived, opioids were often prescribed. The ill effects weren't known then.

In the early 1900s, about 1 in 200 Americans was addicted to opioids, most commonly morphine. Use of another opioid, heroin, was also spiking.

People's opinions about opioids changed after that. In the 1800s, addiction mainly affected white people who bought morphine from doctors. Society considered it to be a tragedy. Then, the people who used it began to change. Immigrant men were the most visible users. Now, people began to think of addiction as a crime. They regarded the drugs as dangerous. In response, the U.S. government passed a series of acts to curb the usage of opioids. One was the Harrison Narcotic Control Act in 1914. Instead of caring for those with addiction, authorities now sent them to prison.

Growing in the field, poppies look perfectly harmless—and lovely.

As laws about drug use became tougher, doctors became more cautious about prescribing them. They feared that patients were likely to abuse the drugs or become addicted. So they rarely prescribed them, even for those with severe pain. Doctors also encouraged cancer patients to stay off opioids until their lives "could be measured in weeks."

What Are Opioids?

Healthcare professionals were right to be cautious. Opioids are extremely effective at reducing pain, but they are also extremely addictive.

Humans have opioid receptors throughout their nervous systems. These receptors regulate the pain and reward systems in our bodies. An opioid is a substance that acts on these opioid receptors.

Opioid receptors got their name from opium, the original opioid. Opium is obtained from a kind of poppy. Humans have been using it for thousands of years. After opium, people made other drugs from the poppy plant that act in similar ways. First there was morphine. Then heroin. After that came oxycodone, hydrocodone, and others. These were used in new prescription medicines such as Vicodin, Percocet, and OxyContin. All these drugs derived from poppies are a specific type of opioid known as opiates.

There are also synthetic (laboratory-created) drugs that act just like opiates but are not derived from the plant. They include fentanyl and methadone. These synthetic drugs are opioids, but not opiates. All opioids have a powerful effect on people's pain-and-reward systems.

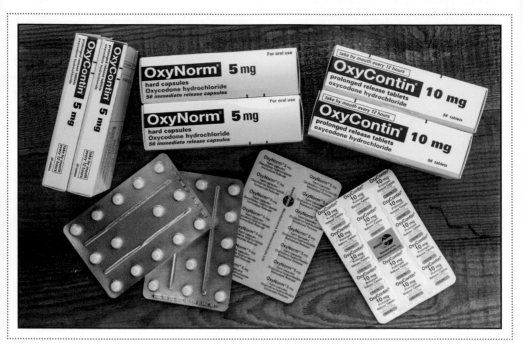

Oxycodone goes by several names. By any and all, it is addictive.

A Push for Pain Management

As the 20th century went on, the addiction crisis of the early 1900s faded from memory. Starting in the 1970s, opinions in the medical field slowly began to change again. Researchers published studies that showed doctors were not doing enough to help patients manage pain, especially at the end of life. Their research showed that patients could take opioids to relieve their pain. If they took the drugs under the careful supervision of a doctor, some researchers claimed, there was only a very small chance that they would become addicted.

In 1986, the World Health Organization released a detailed study. It said that postoperative pain and cancer pain were undertreated. In the following years, several publications echoed that assertion. Advocacy groups including the American Pain Foundation joined the discussion in the 1990s. They argued that high-strength painkillers such as opioids should be prescribed more often for patients with more kinds of pain. The argument, basically, was this: If patients have moderate to severe pain, and we can help relieve that pain, then we should. They argued that it was inhumane not to do so. Many pain specialists pushed the idea that opioids were not addictive if they were used to treat pain.

But there was a problem with this newfound interest in pain management. Those studies cited from the 1970s were too small and not rigorous enough to draw conclusions. And most of the writers who had argued for opioids to manage pain were specialists whose patients suffered the pain of end-stage cancer. Addiction is not a concern at the end of life. Bur there are many kinds of chronic pain that are not fatal, for which addiction is a real risk.

In short, arguments about the safety of opioids were not supported by scientific evidence. One pain specialist later admitted as much. "Because the primary goal was to destigmatize, we often left evidence behind," he said.

Nevertheless, the push for better pain management continued. In 2000, The Joint Commission (TJC) published standards for pain management. These emphasized the need to assess and treat pain. TJC is an organization that accredits more than 21,000 healthcare organizations in the United States. Most states require hospitals and clinics to have accreditation from TJC to get reimbursement from Medicare or Medicaid, health insurance paid by the government. So the organization's recommendations carried a lot of weight. What healthcare providers likely did not know was that TJC was funded by drug companies. The standards it put forth were essentially written by Purdue Pharma, the maker of OxyContin.

Around the same time, government agencies such as the Drug Enforcement Agency said that they would not strictly regulate physicians who prescribed opioids. Doctors previously may have been worried about legal consequences if their patients abused opioids. Now, they felt freer to prescribe them. In fact, because of TJC's mandate to better manage pain in patients, they were *encouraged* to prescribe them. The alternative— letting patients suffer pain—was now considered cruel and unprofessional.

In the 1990s and beyond, the Drug Enforcement Agency was much more focused on catching criminals who smuggled heroin into the U.S. than on regulating American doctors prescribing opioids.

By the late 1990s, medical schools had already begun teaching students to treat pain with opioids—and only with opioids. Other forms of pain therapy—such as massage, relaxation, physical therapy, and biofeedback—were ignored.

Drug Companies Step Up Pressure

Pharmaceutical companies had been leading the chorus of voices arguing that opioids were not only humane but also safe. They hired consultants to speak about the benefits and safety of opioids. They directed their sales representatives to pressure doctors to prescribe their pills at high doses and for long periods of time. They also gave massive funding to advocacy and professional organizations such as the American Pain Foundation and TJC. This influenced the organizations to strongly support increased opioid prescribing.

Drug companies also began producing new types of pills, such as extended release oxycodone (OxyContin). The companies claimed that these new pills were even less likely to be abused than previous opioids. The reason, they said, was that they released opioids gradually into the system. The companies claimed that patients didn't experience the extreme highs and lows that typically led to addiction. But in truth, the pills were highly addictive and widely abused.

Fact

OxyContin prescriptions spiked from 670,000 to 6.2 million between 1997 and 2002.

All these changes led to an increase in opioid prescriptions. In 2000, patients consumed 46,946 kilograms (103,498 pounds) of opioids. By 2012, usage had reached 165,525 kg (364,920 lb.). By then, doctors were prescribing powerful painkillers even after routine surgeries such as appendectomies. They were also using pills to treat chronic conditions such as moderate to severe back pain. Previously, chronic pain had been treated through a variety of strategies. These only sometimes included drugs. Now, drugs were essentially the only treatment.

For a while, the change seemed to be having a positive effect. Patients gave higher satisfaction ratings to hospitals that used more opioids for treatment. Patients reported less pain with no obvious side effects.

Stephanie Price sits behind a photo of her son, Jeromy Bubacz, who died of an overdose of prescription drugs. They were initially prescribed to him after surgery for a lung condition so serious that he was discharged from the U.S. Marine Corps when it was discovered.

But there were problems. A huge number of people were becoming addicted to painkillers. If they couldn't get pills through legal means, many turned to illegal ("street") drugs. It turned out that opioids were extremely dangerous. What's more, the drug companies had known it all along.

Addicted Doctors

Patients weren't the only ones starting to take opioids in large amounts. Doctors, too, began taking pills. After all, they had pain, just like anyone else. But they also had something most patients didn't have—easy access to drugs.

Lou Ortenzio of Clarksville, West Virginia, was one such doctor. He was working late one night in 1988, seeing patients well after regular office hours. He was a popular doctor in the small town. He worked hard to give all his patients the personal attention he felt they deserved. But that meant he often worked very long days. On this particular night, the stress and tension had given him a bad headache.

To relieve the pain, Ortenzio took an extra-strength Vicodin. The pill contains acetaminophen (the main ingredient in Tylenol) and hydrocodone, an opioid painkiller. It was a free sample left behind by a drug company representative. It did the trick to relieve the doctor's headache—and then some.

"It was a feeling like I'd never felt before," he later said. The tension, pain, and anxiety melted away. He felt great.

Over the years, Ortenzio took more and more Vicodin. By the end of 1999, he was taking up to 30 pills a day. The free samples couldn't cover his needs. To get more pills, he began to write prescriptions in other people's names but kept the drugs for himself. In 2006, he was convicted of healthcare fraud. He lost his medical license. He was left unemployed.

Forced to start over, Ortenzio got a job delivering pizzas. But eventually, he found meaning by helping other people get help for their addictions.

CHAPTER THREE

The **Cycle**

By the year 2000, the town of Portsmouth, Ohio, was deep in the throes of an epidemic. Once a thriving industrial center, it had been declining for decades. Now, instead of products for sale, an empty storefront displayed memorials to those who had died of overdose.

An organization located in Portsmouth, Ohio, that seeks to end substance abuse memorializes local victims of drug abuse and drug-related violence.

In Ohio as a whole, fatal overdoses had more than quadrupled over the past decade. In Portsmouth, 1 in 10 babies was born with drugs already in his or her system. One family, the Mannerings, had seen OxyContin beginning to rip apart the community. The parents wanted to protect their high school–aged children. So, they talked to neighbors and asked them to please stop selling drugs. But dealers were peddling pills from 11 houses on their road alone. One dealer was a woman in her 70s.

Despite the efforts of the Mannering parents, their children, Nina and Chad, became addicted while still in high school. Chad served three years in prison for robbery, but then he achieved sobriety.

Nina was not so lucky. She tried to quit, but in January 2010, at age 29, she was killed. She was staying with someone who had access to prescriptions when a man broke into the house. The intruder was looking for pills. He shot them both. Nina's 8-year-old daughter witnessed the murder. Nina's mother added her daughter's picture to the memorial images in the store window.

More Prescriptions, More Demand

The story of the Mannerings was just one of many like it. Towns with problems like Portsmouth's were becoming common all over the country. Between 2003 and 2018, opioid prescriptions in the United States quadrupled. So did deaths due to opioids.

Doctors aggressively prescribing painkillers had created the conditions for an epidemic. A cycle started when doctors prescribed painkillers such as OxyContin to patients with chronic pain. If the patients had a history of addiction, they might develop an addiction to the pills. More often, those pills got into the hands of others, such as family members or friends, who were not prescribed them. These users were more likely to develop an addiction.

Many doctors were alarmed at the rates of addiction they saw in their patients. They refused to renew prescriptions. But some doctors illegally sold or traded prescriptions for money or sex. Others were themselves addicted. They used their connections to get more drugs. In many areas, law enforcement saw the devastation that pills were causing in their communities. Police cracked down on "pill mills," doctors illegally distributing prescription painkillers.

In Florida in 2011, Dr. Zvi Harry Perper was arrested after his Delray Beach clinic was raided by Drug Enforcement Agency officers as a pill mill.

The crackdown created the next step in the cycle. When people addicted to opioids could no longer get pills from doctors, they tried to buy them illegally. Of the more than 97 million people who took prescription painkillers in 2015, 12 million of them did so without a prescription.

A young woman watches as her boyfriend is taken into custody in Hillsborough County, Florida, for possession of heroin.

Just as the population of people addicted to opioids was spiking, access to legal prescription painkillers was shrinking. At the same time, street opioids such as heroin were becoming easier to find. That created conditions for the next step in the cycle. Users graduated from prescription pills to street drugs.

That increased the risk of overdose and other problems. People have no assurance about what is in the drugs they buy illegally. Of course, the world of drug dealers and users is itself a dangerous one. The combination of intense addiction and large amounts of cash creates an atmosphere of desperation and violence. Opioid addiction can be treated. But if it is not, the end of the cycle may be death.

Yet through all this, there still has been no reliable study showing that treating chronic pain with opioids is effective—or safe—over the long term. On the contrary, the pills were making things worse for patients, even outside of addiction risks. Some patients became hypersensitive to pain. Others experienced increased disability. Many developed problems with their glands, as well as psychological challenges. Long-term opioid therapy is useful for severe pain. But the damaging side effects mean it should be a treatment of last resort for people with chronic pain.

Fact

Drug overdoses are now the leading cause of death for Americans under 50. Drug deaths are rising faster than ever. From 2015 to 2016, drug overdose rates from synthetic opioids doubled.

Affecting All Types

More and more people were getting caught up in the deadly epidemic. The highest overdose rates have been in Appalachia, the Rust Belt, and New England. But these trends are changing quickly. White people have been the most affected demographic so far, likely because they have had the best access to medical care. That means they were the ones being prescribed opioids. But that too is changing, as street drugs such as heroin spread.

The negative effects go beyond overdoses, which are simply the most visible and easiest to track. Data from 2015 showed that more than 2 million Americans had a problem with opioids, including addiction. And they were all kinds of people—workers and business owners, parents and teenagers, rich and poor.

Veterans were one population hit particularly hard. Soldiers were returning from tours in Iraq and Afghanistan with chronic pain and, all too often, post-traumatic stress disorder (PTSD). The Department of Veterans Affairs and the Department of Defense had regulations meant to reduce prescribing opioids for veterans and active soldiers. Even so, many doctors were relying on opioids to treat these conditions. Evidence has shown that veterans with these conditions are more likely to use the drugs in risky ways. They're also more likely to have negative outcomes such as overdoses and self-inflicted injuries.

Addiction has hit veterans hard. Many are homeless because of it. In Minneapolis, people have pitched tents next to the highway. Navy veteran Jim, 64, proudly flew the U.S. flag outside his shelter.

Many doctors associated with veterans' affairs were working to treat pain and PTSD with therapies other than drugs. These included acupuncture, chiropractic care, physical therapy, and exercise therapy. Relaxation exercises and psychological therapies were other options.

But general practitioners are typically not experts in treating PTSD. These doctors may prescribe opioids because these drugs are the easiest and quickest way to ease their patients' suffering.

That was true for all types of patients, not only veterans. Doctors had little time—or training—to address pain in more nuanced ways. A pill could make the pain go away now. Pills didn't only save time. More and more, they were what patients wanted. They were also what insurance companies, professional organizations, and hospitals wanted.

Fact

It is estimated that one in five combat veterans reports symptoms of PTSD. Chronic pain is also common. That's true even for soldiers who have not been injured in battle. The day-to-day work of being a soldier is hard on the body. The simple acts of carrying heavy equipment and wearing body armor can lead to back, knee, and other joint pain.

Private Pain in Public

Painkillers were destroying families, but the damage was not confined to the privacy of people's homes. The misery of pain and loss played out in some very public ways. Celebrities such as the provocative radio pundit Rush Limbaugh went through public struggles. His ordeal with addiction and treatment was scrutinized and reported on. Pro wrestler Axl Rotten overdosed and died in a McDonald's restroom. Super Bowl champion quarterback Brett Favre admitted in an interview that he played his MVP season in 1995 while taking as many as 14 Vicodin pills a day.

When Brett Favre was a football hero, no one knew he was relying on pain pills to make it through his games.

Many ordinary people went through their struggles in public as well. Going through withdrawal, they were desperate to use opioids. So they did so wherever they could, often in public.

They overdosed and died in public areas as well. Police officers regularly found drug users either unconscious or dead. They were in cars, in public bathrooms, on buses and subways, and in hospitals, parks, and libraries.

A medic gives naloxone to a 32-year-old man who had overdosed on heroin.

By 2016, about 125 people a day were dying from drug overdoses. Of those, 78 were overdoses from heroin and painkillers. Many more than that would have died but were revived from the edge of death. Police or others saved them with naloxone, a drug that reverses the effects of opioid overdose. These near-death experiences, too, often took place in public places.

Drug Companies Keep Pushing Opioids

The dangers of opioids had become obvious by the early 2000s. Even patients who did not become addicted sometimes suffered negative side effects. These included sleep apnea, reduced hormone production, and impaired motor skills. The elderly fell more frequently and broke bones when they were on too heavy a dose of opioids. But the most severe dangers were clearly a matter of life and death. Doctors could see this in their practices. The CDC urged doctors to be more careful about using painkillers.

Most large pharmaceutical companies have well-paid sales representatives. They are in the business of persuading doctors to prescribe their brands of pills.

Some doctors did become more cautious about prescribing pills. But the majority continued to prescribe at a high rate. One reason was that it was an easy and seemingly effective way to ease patients' pain. Another reason is that drug companies were pressuring them.

Drug companies have always spent huge amounts of money to market their products to physicians.

Opioids at the Hospital

Patients should be able to assume they are being taken care of safely when they're in healthcare centers. Yet even there, many patients were being overprescribed opioids. One study looked at the rate of patients being oversedated—given doses of opioids so high that they struggled to remain conscious and sometimes to breathe. The rate more than doubled when doctors followed new pain management standards. It went from 11.0 per 100,000 inpatient hospital days to 24.5. The rate of people who died from not breathing also went up.

Representatives visit doctors and woo them with free dinners, paid trips, and more. When these companies started marketing opioid painkillers more intensively in the mid-1990s, they used these same tactics. In fact, they more than doubled their efforts. In 1995, drug companies had about 38,000 representatives making calls on doctors. Ten years later, the number was about 100,000.

These sales reps worked to convince doctors that opioids were the best way to help patients cope with pain. They offered doctors small items, such as mugs and fishing hats. They also gave lavish gifts such as all-expenses-paid stays at fancy resorts.

Almost from the beginning, the companies knew these drugs were not safe. But they marketed them aggressively anyway.

That marketing appears to have been very successful in increasing sales. The number of prescriptions issued in 2015 was triple the number issued in 1999, research showed. One study looked at the money these companies spent in individual counties. It compared the money spent

on marketing to the amount of opioids prescribed. It also looked at the number of opioid-related deaths. The results were stark. The counties that got more marketing in a given year saw more painkiller prescriptions the following year. They also saw more overdose deaths.

In recent years, the number of opioid prescriptions has gone down slightly. But according to one study, doctors who receive perks from drug companies have not followed suit. Their opioid prescriptions went up.

Researchers pointed out that the link was not necessarily causal. In other words, getting perks might not be leading directly to more prescriptions. It might be the other way around. Doctors who give out more prescriptions may get more rewards from drug companies. Either way, the upshot was that doctors were being rewarded for prescribing more opioids. It didn't matter whether opioids were a good choice for the patients. The result was a country swept up in a wave of addiction.

Frequency of Heroin Use and Heroin-Related Deaths in the United States, 2000–2015

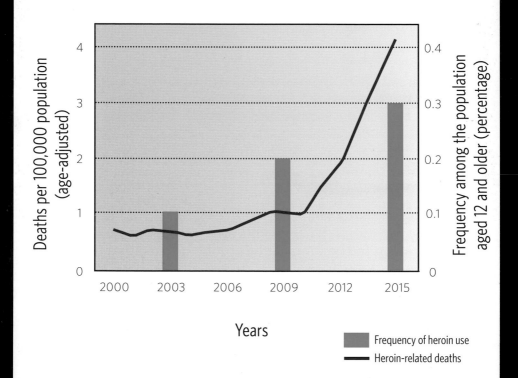

Source: http://www.unodc.org/wdr2017/field/Booklet_3_Plantbased_drugs.pdf

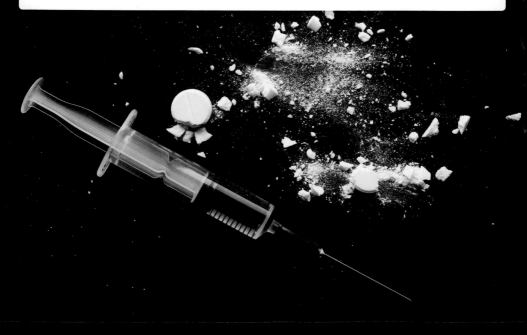

The cultivation of drugs is a huge industry in Afghanistan. This 8-year-old child had already learned to harvest the opium poppies in his father's field.

Production of Heroin

Why was heroin becoming so easy to find? Simply put, people were making more of it. In 2016 alone, the total area worldwide that was being used to grow poppies for opiates increased by 8 percent. The total was about 304,800 hectares (753,177 acres). That's about the size of 427,000 soccer fields, all dedicated to producing drugs. About two thirds of heroin was being cultivated in Afghanistan. In all, about 448 tons (406 tonnes) of heroin was produced that year.

The increased production helped drive down its price. Increased distribution made it easier to purchase the drug in communities such as suburbs and rural areas. Customers were already waiting there. When the supply of prescription opioids was cut back in the 2010s, many people with addiction were desperate for an alternative supply. Illegal heroin markets provided it to them.

CHAPTER FOUR

The **Third Wave**

The opioid epidemic in the United States came in three waves. The first wave started in the 1990s, when doctors started prescribing more opioid painkillers. They were urged to do so by faulty research and federal guidelines arguing for stronger pain management. Drug companies' aggressive marketing of their drugs was a big factor too.

This, in turn, led to abuse and addiction. One study found that about 8 percent of people who take prescription opioids for chronic pain become addicted. And up to 26 percent behave in ways that doctors say are unhealthy. These behaviors aren't the same as addiction. But they might include people taking more pills than they are supposed to in order to get high. Some patients aggressively pestered doctors for prescriptions.

With all those prescriptions out there, the drugs became widely available. People using the pills included not only the patients themselves but also their friends and families. That included teens who took the drugs from their parents as well as people who bought excess pills illegally. In fact, the most common source of pills for people who misused them was a friend or relative.

The second wave came in the early 2000s. By this time, there was a huge population of people using opioids who had lost access to prescription pills. That's when heroin began to flood the illegal drug market. It filled that void in big cities, suburbs, and rural areas. People hooked on pills turned in large numbers to heroin. It was cheaper than pills. Because of tighter regulations on prescriptions, it was also easier to get.

Michael, a young man in the South Bronx, is just one of many addicted to heroin. More than 1,370 New York City residents died from overdoses in 2016. Most of those deaths involved opioids.

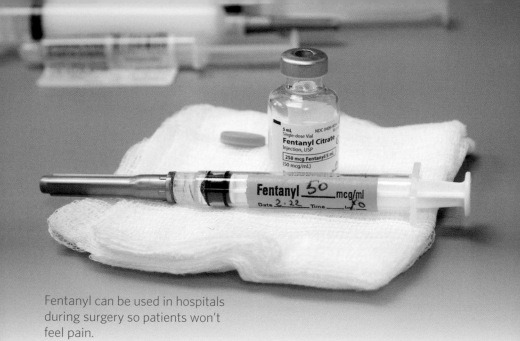

Fentanyl can be used in hospitals during surgery so patients won't feel pain.

Synthetic Drugs

Most recently, a third wave has hit the country. This is the wave of fentanyl, a synthetic alternative to heroin that is cheaper—and far more potent.

Fentanyl's strength makes it far deadlier than other drugs. Even a tiny error in measurement can lead to an overdose. Worse, drugs bought illegally aren't regulated. That means the contents of those drugs can change frequently. This makes it easy for people to underestimate the strength of the drug they are taking.

Some users seek out fentanyl, but more often, people don't know they are taking it. Some illegal drug makers mix fentanyl into other drugs because it is less expensive. Users may think they are taking a certain drug, such as cocaine, heroin, or a prescription pill. But they're actually getting fentanyl.

Like other opioids, fentanyl is available by prescription. It was originally produced by a pharmaceutical company in 1959. It was used as an anesthetic during surgery and a pain reliever. In the 1990s, a fentanyl patch was introduced that patients could wear to treat chronic pain. From there, more methods of taking fentanyl were created. There was even a lollipop.

But most fentanyl on the streets today is made illegally. China is the biggest producer of the drug. Drugs are not regulated as strictly there. So, China produces many drugs that are illegal in other countries. Chinese fentanyl is smuggled into the United States directly from China as well as

Fact

One research report described a woman who abused fentanyl patches by wearing the prescribed amount while also chewing up to four patches a day. She said the combination made her feel euphoric. She later went into treatment for addiction.

through Mexico. And it is spreading quickly. U.S. border agents seized about 8 lbs. (3.6 kg) of fentanyl in 2014. One year later, they seized about 200 lbs. (90 kg).

This third wave caused a spike in overdose deaths. The CDC released a report showing that more than 28,000 people died from a synthetic opioid overdose in 2017. That number was up from 3,000 in 2013. It brought the total number of overdose deaths in the United States to more than 70,000 in 2017.

One problem is that the synthetic drugs are so strong that more of the anti-overdose medication naloxone must be used to save lives. An official in Warren County, Ohio, has seen it happen over and over. One hit of naloxone

The Zone is a community in Marietta, Georgia, for those in recovery from opioid and alcohol addiction. It was started by Missy and Michael Owen in 2016 after the drug-overdose death of their 20-year-old son, Davis. These men are members of a support group there.

against a fentanyl overdose was like "a squirt gun in a house fire," he said.

This shows how powerful addiction can be. Even if they know the risks, even if fentanyl might be in their drugs, people use it anyway.

Powerful Enough to Knock Out an Elephant

Another synthetic opioid is carfentanil, an elephant tranquilizer. Carfentanil is 5,000 times stronger than heroin. An amount less than a few grains of salt can kill a person. The drug is so powerful, it changed a city in one day. A narcotics unit police commander in Akron, Ohio, remembers it well. "July 5, 2016," said police captain Michael Shearer. "That's the day carfentanil hit the streets of Akron." That day, 17 people overdosed and one person died in the span of nine hours. Over the next six months, 140 people died of carfentanil overdoses.

National Drug Overdose Deaths by Drug Type, 1999 to 2017

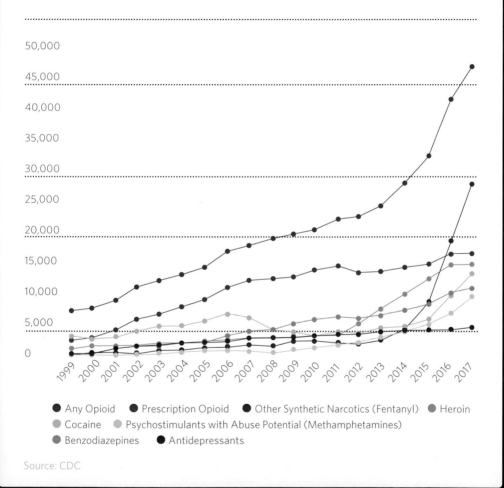

- ● Any Opioid
- ● Prescription Opioid
- ● Other Synthetic Narcotics (Fentanyl)
- ● Heroin
- ● Cocaine
- ● Psychostimulants with Abuse Potential (Methamphetamines)
- ● Benzodiazepines
- ● Antidepressants

Source: CDC

CHAPTER FIVE

The **Response**

The response to the opioid epidemic has played out in different ways in different arenas.

Public Health Measures

Inevitably, doctors, government health officials, and lawmakers began to take notice of the crisis. Doctors started cutting back on prescriptions, and the total number of prescriptions began to fall in 2012, though the number is still much higher than it was in 1999. And the number of overdose deaths continued to rise because of nonprescription drugs such as heroin and fentanyl.

In 2016, the U.S. Food and Drug Administration (FDA) began approving new opioids that would deter abuse. That year, it also called for greater access to naloxone and stronger warnings on pill containers. The Joint Commission (TJC) drafted new public standards in 2017. Its pain management standards from the year 2000 had helped prompt the beginning of the drug crisis. These new standards outline "a multi-level approach to pain management to help frontline staff and clinicians deliver safe, individualized pain care."

On October 26, 2017, the U.S. government declared the opioid epidemic a public health emergency. The declaration gave the U.S. Department of Health and Human Services increased flexibility to spend funds on the issue. It didn't provide *more* funding, so it didn't have a practical effect on the crisis. But it did help draw the nation's attention to the severity of the crisis.

On October 26, 2017, while many looked on, President Donald Trump signed an executive order declaring the opioid epidemic a public health emergency. Two years later, not much had been done to stem the crisis.

Attitude of the General Public

At least 2.1 million U.S. residents have an opioid addiction. So, a good many Americans didn't need a federal declaration to make them aware of it. They, their friends, or their family members struggle with addiction every day.

Still, for many Americans, the crisis was an abstract idea. It may have crossed their awareness when they heard about high-profile celebrities grappling with addiction. Actors Matthew Perry and Charlie Sheen and rappers Macklemore and Eminem were four examples. Other examples included singer and former child actor Demi Lovato and rock stars Courtney Love and Steven Tyler. *Glee* star Cory Monteith died of an overdose in 2013.

Even child stars such as Demi Lovato were not exempt from addiction. In 2018, Lovato overdosed on oxycodone laced with fentanyl and had to be revived with naloxone. She went into rehab and recovered.

In April 2016, opioids took the life of Prince, one of the biggest rock stars in history. He had been taking opioids for years to alleviate pain in his hips. The pain came

When Prince died from an overdose of fentanyl in 2016, his death shocked the world.

from decades of dancing in high-heeled shoes. The drug he overdosed on was fentanyl. A year and a half later, the same drug killed another legendary singer, Tom Petty. He had been using opioids to manage pain from a fractured hip while he was touring.

The fact that this crisis has mostly affected white people may have helped inspire a more forgiving attitude. Society has taken a public health–oriented approach. Compare this to past drug crises, which largely affected people of color. The epidemics of heroin in the 1960s and 1970s and crack cocaine in the 1980s drew much less compassion from mainstream news and government officials. The United States responded with a "war on drugs" that included zero tolerance for offenses and stiff prison sentences.

Another factor is that Americans tend to see the epidemic as being the fault of doctors overprescribing painkillers. They may perceive those who have gotten hooked on opioids as victims.

Pharmaceutical Companies Held Responsible

There was less sympathy for the drug companies that pushed opioids for years. These companies include Purdue Pharma, Endo, Teva, and Abbott Laboratories, among others. They exaggerated the benefits of opioids and downplayed the risks. They supported so-called "education" campaigns that encouraged widespread use of opioids. They also lobbied lawmakers to loosen access to the drugs.

This Purdue Pharma facility in Wilson, North Carolina, was long a manufacturing hub for OxyContin.

Some Purdue staff warned their bosses about overprescribing and illegal pill mills. This should have been reported to federal officials. But the company ignored the warnings. All these actions played an outsized role in creating the epidemic.

Eventually, the companies were hit with lawsuits seeking to hold them responsible for that role. Purdue Pharma paid more than $630 million in federal fines for deceptive marketing in 2007. Three executives were sentenced to three years of probation and 400 hours of community service. And they admitted that they had misrepresented the addictive nature of their opioid, OxyContin.

Purdue Pharma was also the subject of a host of other investigations and lawsuits. Yet the company continued to market OxyContin aggressively. It went further in 2014, when it developed a new business plan. As the addiction crisis the company helped create got worse, it decided to make even more money by selling treatment for addiction. "Pain treatment and addiction are naturally linked," said one company document that was obtained by the state of New York. It went on to describe the strategy as a way that Purdue could be an "end-to-end pain provider." The company made money from pain treatment *and* from addiction treatment.

Families filled the courtroom while protesters outside held up posters of beloved family members and friends who had died of opioid overdoses.

More recently, more lawsuits have been filed against Purdue and the family that runs it. The Sackler family has been highly involved in the operations of its company. A filing in Massachusetts exposed how Purdue's president, Richard Sackler, was personally involved in decisions to recklessly push OxyContin.

Other states filing suit against the family include New York, Connecticut, Rhode Island, and Utah. Various other legal claims targeted Purdue as well. They also went after other manufacturers, distributors, and pharmacy chains. By the end of 2017, about 1,600 cases had been brought on behalf of cities, counties, American Indian tribes, hospitals, and others. The cases represented millions of people. There were so many lawsuits that a federal judge in Cleveland bundled them together into one giant suit.

In September 2019, Purdue reached a temporary settlement that would provide more than $10 billion for the opioid crisis. The company filed for bankruptcy to do so, but admitted no responsibility for the crisis. The other suits are still pending.

Progress Made Locally

Changes made at the federal level, such as TJC's new standards, may have varying effects on the crisis. Over the past few years, Congress has written several bills, such as the Synthetic Drug Awareness Act, meant to help. But experts say that, as a whole, these bills fall short of what needs to happen to effectively address the epidemic.

The greatest progress has been made at the state and local level. The fixes are not as grand or sweeping as declaring a national health emergency. But they make real-life differences. Nonprofit organizations set up needle exchanges (to prevent transmission of disease) or distribute naloxone. Some lobby lawmakers or provide safe spaces to recover from or get treatment for addiction. Health clinics provide methadone or buprenorphine for people who want to end their opioid addiction. Most states have set up monitoring systems that make sure patients are not getting prescriptions from multiple doctors.

Some activists and state and local health departments have begun using harm reduction strategies to great effect. *Harm reduction* refers to strategies and ideas that reduce the negative consequences of drug use. The belief at the heart of harm reduction is that those who use drugs are human beings with a disease. Drug addiction is real, and to help people, we need to meet them "where they are." This is different from the more traditional view of thinking of those who use drugs as criminals and focusing on punishing them.

Harm-reduction advocates work to get users access to clean syringes. This prevents diseases that can be passed through dirty ones. They advocate for greater access to naloxone. They push for medication-assisted treatment for those addicted to opioids. They educate community and state leaders on how to reduce the risk of overdose. One way that is done is by providing safe places to use the drugs. These efforts lead to more people getting the chance to stop using. The impact of the opioid crisis is reduced.

A similar change has come in police departments. In many areas, police are doing more than simply locking up drug offenders. They are helping them get treatment. Eric Adams, for example, is a former undercover narcotics officer in New Hampshire. He said he has changed his view on responding to drug abusers. "I can't tell you what changed inside of me," he said. "But these are people and they have a purpose in life and we can't as law enforcement look at them any other way. They are committing crimes to feed their addiction, plain and simple. They need help."

In places such as Vermont, Pennsylvania, Massachusetts, and Ohio, police investigate heroin deaths with the same intensity they would a homicide. The intent is not only to track down dealers or other criminals. The police also want to get a better handle on what is happening in their cities. Then, they can issue warnings about deadly strains of drugs. They can help vulnerable users. Many officers give people arrested for drug possession a choice between treatment and jail.

In some towns, police work closely with social services providers to more effectively approach homes with drug problems. Rutland, Vermont, is an example. The town has multiple agencies working together to identify homes where drugs are a problem. Instead of waiting for someone to get hurt or a law to be broken, they intervene to connect drug users with appropriate treatment *before* something bad happens. The governor has directed money to Rutland to get certain drug abusers quickly into treatment instead of into jail.

Fact

Many police departments have made naloxone a standard part of their equipment. States like New York are directing funds so that all officers are trained and equipped with the lifesaving medication.

In 2016, the government announced it would tear down a building believed to have been used as a drug house and give it to a nonprofit group to rehabilitate. The group built a park where the house had been.

The shift from punishing to helping can be heard in the words of Joy Malek Oldfield of Akron, Ohio. A judge in drug court, Oldfield is providing praise and a supportive voice to offenders who come through her courtroom. "When you get sober, it's not just rainbows and unicorns," she told one young defendant. "But it's a better life, don't you think?" Messages like that acknowledge the challenges people with addiction face, but also come across as encouraging. They can give people the hope and support they need to get clean.

What Else Can Be Done?

There is no easy fix to the opioid crisis. Solutions will have to come in many forms. For now, there are two things we can change to help fight the crisis. One is how we manage pain so fewer people get addicted. The other is how we treat people who do get addicted.

Changing how the U.S. medical system manages pain will be key. Opioid painkillers improve the quality of life for millions of people, so we can't simply stop prescribing them altogether. In particular, cancer patients and those with acute pain rely on opioids. But in general, doctors need to prescribe lower doses, for shorter periods of time. A more holistic approach to pain treatment would cut down the need for opioids.

We need to reduce the supply of prescription opioids being used recreationally while still providing enough access for those who need them. We do not want stricter regulations to block patients who are in genuine need. One solution may be to use state prescription drug–monitoring programs to alert officials to pill mills or people getting multiple prescriptions from different doctors. This can help us identify people who may need addiction treatment.

The drug crisis began with drug companies aggressively marketing their pills. Given that, restrictions on the marketing of drugs, or stricter regulation of the pharmaceutical industry, would be an important step.

For those who are already addicted, it's important to have treatment easily available. That means being

This Bradenton, Florida, man has struggled for years to kick his addiction to prescription opioids. For many years, he has been enrolled in a methadone clinic, gradually reducing his dose. He hopes to be able to leave the program for good soon and live on his own.

proactive and finding people who need treatment instead of waiting for them to seek treatment themselves.

Addiction treatment also needs to be robust. Counseling and inpatient clinics are helpful. But the most effective treatment for opioid addiction often requires medications like methadone or buprenorphine. These synthetic drugs act similarly to morphine and are effective in helping people wean off of heroin.

Other treatments, such as "tough love" programs, are actually harmful and damaging. These programs punish people for using and may isolate users from friends and family. They often result in people using more drugs to cope with the pain of being shut out and punished. Programs like this should be avoided. People perform their best when they are supported and given positive, nonjudgmental advice.

The opioid epidemic is the worst drug crisis in U.S. history. In the end, it may be that the sheer size and scope will lead to the crisis finally being solved. It has affected so many people, and so many types of people, that it's impossible to ignore. Americans deserve solutions. And they are demanding them.

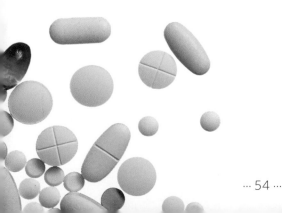

White Influence

Opioid abuse has wreaked havoc in all demographics, but it has hit whites especially hard. Many of the families affected live in suburbs and small towns. These are middle-class people with privilege and influence. And they are using those to shape the perception of—and approach to—the opioid crisis.

When Courtney Griffin was using heroin, her family did everything they could to keep her out of trouble and her problem a secret. She lied and stole from family members. She spent $400 a day on heroin. But her family paid her debts and never got the police involved. It wasn't until she died at age 20 of an overdose that they finally admitted publicly what had happened to her.

The Griffins used their influence while Courtney was alive to try to protect her. After she died, they used it to help others. They testified at hearings and forums, and they talked to other parents dealing with the same problem. They also worked directly to help people with addictions. They hosted dinners at a church for them and their families. And they worked to create a safe, sober house for drug users and their families. They named it for their daughter.

Affluent families are lobbying statehouses, holding rallies, and starting nonprofit organizations. Their efforts have helped shape the nation's efforts to address the crisis.

Many people have pointed out the stark difference to the harsh way the U.S. government dealt with crack, which mostly affected black communities. A more compassionate approach then could have reduced the devastating mass incarceration of black men. The difference is distressing. Still, most agree that compassion is a welcome change. It may hold the key to solving the crisis.

GET INVOLVED

The staggering toll of the opioid crisis can make many people feel helpless. What can one person possibly do to end or even slow down the crisis—or help individuals affected by it? As a young person, you may feel especially unqualified to help. But in fact, there are steps you can take. One of the most important ways of getting involved is to spread awareness of the facts of the opioid crisis.

Now that you understand some of the history of the crisis, and the ways it affects people of all ages and backgrounds, you can use your voice to help others learn more about this important issue. Whether you personally know people who suffer from opioid addiction or have been moved by stories you've heard, there are several ways you can get involved.

Here are some suggestions:

1. Talk to your family about safely storing and disposing of medications. It's estimated that two thirds of teens and young adults who abuse prescription medication first found the drugs at the home of friends or family members. So, keeping medicine out of reach can have a big impact. Ask your family members if they have a safe place to keep prescription medicine, and how they plan to dispose of it when they no longer need it.
If they don't have a plan in place, you can explain that it's important to keep medicine in a secure place in the house and to participate in a safe drug disposal program. Safe disposal programs include community programs and mail-back programs.

Tell your family members that they can visit the American Medicine Chest Challenge to learn more or find a take-back location near them.

2. If you personally know someone who's struggling with addiction, you can encourage him or her to find help and support. The Partnership for Drug-Free Kids has a helpline, and they offer support and advice to families and friends of young people with addictions. People needing support can call 855-378-4373 or text 55753. You can learn about harm reduction strategies at the website of the Harm Reduction Coalition (https://harmreduction.org).

3. Call or write your local, state, and federal representatives to ask for support for addiction resources. The federal government passed the Substance Use-Disorder Prevention That Promotes Opioid Recovery and Treatment (SUPPORT) for Patients and Communities Act in October 2018. You can write to your U.S. senators and representatives to ask what other legislation they are considering to help end the opioid crisis.

4. If you're on social media, you can use your platform to spread awareness. One place to find videos to share is the Partnership for Drug-Free Kids' YouTube channel (https://www.youtube.com/user/drugfreechannel).

GLOSSARY

biofeedback—the technique of controlling things in your body with your conscious mind

fentanyl—a powerful synthetic opioid that is 50 times stronger than heroin

naloxone—a synthetic medication that reverses the effects of opioids and can save someone from an overdose

narcotic—a drug that dulls the senses, relieves pain, and induces profound sleep; high doses can cause severe reactions such as coma or convulsions

opiate—a drug derived from opium

opioid—a narcotic drug, whether natural or synthetic, that acts on opioid receptors that regulate pain and reward systems

opium—a narcotic drug that is derived from poppy plants

pill mill—an operation in which a doctor, clinic, or pharmacy prescribes and/or dispenses narcotics without a legitimate medical purpose

prescription—an instruction written by a doctor that authorizes a patient to be provided with a medicine

synthetic—a drug produced through a chemical process rather than made from a natural source

withdrawal—the symptoms someone experiences when he or she stops using an addictive drug; they can include physical or psychological pain

ADDITIONAL RESOURCES

Further Reading

Duchess, Harris, with John L. Hakala. *The Opioid Crisis.* Minneapolis: ABDO, 2018.

Quinones, Sam. *Dreamland (YA edition): The True Tale of America's Opiate Epidemic.* New York: Bloomsbury YA, 2019.

Sheff, David, and Nic Sheff. *High: Everything You Want to Know About Drugs, Alcohol, and Addiction.* New York: HMH Books for Young Readers, 2019.

Internet Sites

Kelty Mental Health Resource Center: Substance Use
https://keltymentalhealth.ca/substance-use

National Institute on Drug Abuse for Teens
https://teens.drugabuse.gov/

Partnership for Drug-Free Kids
https://drugfree.org/

Critical Thinking Questions

1. The United States has been through several drug crises in its history. Why do you think it was not better prepared to cope with the opioid crisis? What could it do to prevent future crises?

2. How much fault do you think drug companies have for creating the crisis? Do you think they are being held appropriately responsible? If so, why? If not, how do you think they should account for the damage done?

3 Sometimes, doctors have patients they know are abusing pills. If these patients don't get pills from doctors, the doctors know they may seek out illegal drugs on the street. If you knew of a patient with this problem, what would you do? Why?

SOURCE NOTES

p. 5, "They did everything they could. . ." Jared Dillingham, "Prescott Valley Parents Remember Son Killed by Fentanyl, Newspapers Take Action," *azfamily.com*, March 28, 2019, https://www.azfamily.com/news/investigations/opioid_crisis/fentanyl/prescott-valley-parents-remember-son-killed-by-fentanyl-newspapers-take/article_e9bf5f1e-4cec-11e9-a233-d7e8fa99e68a.html

p. 9, "The idea that a developed wealthy nation . . ." Josh Katz and Margot Sanger-Katz, "'The Numbers Are So Staggering.' Overdose Deaths Set a Record Last Year," *The New York Times,* November 29, 2018, https://www.nytimes.com/interactive/2018/11/29/upshot/fentanyl-drug-overdose-deaths.html

p. 10, "Addiction poisoned everything . . ." Lisa Marie Basile, "A Foster Child of the Opioid Epidemic," *The New York Times,* November 24, 2017, https://www.nytimes.com/2017/11/24/well/family/a-foster-child-of-the-opioid-epidemic.html?searchResultPosition=1

p. 10, "I carry that compassion..." Ibid.

p. 13, "could be measured in weeks..." Mark R. Jones, Omar Viswanath, Jacquelin Peck, Alan D. Kaye, Jatinder S. Gill, and Thomas T. Simopoulos, "A Brief History of the Opioid Epidemic and Strategies for Pain Medicine," NCBI, June 2018, https://www.ncbi.nlm.nih.gov/pmc/articles/PMC5993682/

p. 15, "Because the primary goal was to destigmatize . . ." Sam Quinones, "Physicians Get Addicted Too," *The Atlantic,* May 2019, https://www.theatlantic.com/magazine/archive/2019/05/opioid-epidemic-west-virginia-doctor/586036/

p. 19, "It was a feeling like I'd never felt..." Ibid.

p. 38, "a squirt gun in a house fire..." Josh Katz, "Drug Deaths in America Are Rising Faster Than Ever," *The New York Times*, June 5, 2017, https://www.nytimes.com/interactive/2017/06/05/upshot/opioid-epidemic-drug-overdose-deaths-are-rising-faster-than-ever.html?searchResultPosition=1&mtrref=www.nytimes.com&gwh=7DF8D5CD8403F1524FDFD9966AC5471F&gwt=pay&assetType=REGIWALL

p. 38, "That's the day carfentanil hit the streets…" Josh Katz, "Drug Deaths in America Are Rising Faster Than Ever."

p. 41, "a multi-level approach to pain…" The Joint Commission, "Pain Management Standards—Hospital," January 1, 2018, https://www. jointcommission.org/topics/pain_management_standards_hospital. aspx

p. 46, "Pain treatment and addiction are…" Hakim et al., "Lawsuits Lay Bare Sackler Family's Role in Opioid Crisis," *New York Times,* April 1, 2019.

p. 49, "but these are people…" Katharine Q. Seelye, "In Heroin Crisis, White Families Seek Gentler War on Drugs." *New York Times,* October 30, 2015, https://www.nytimes.com/2015/10/31/us/heroin-war-on-drugs-parents.html?searchResultPosition=1

p. 51, "When you get sober…" Ibid.

All internet sites accessed August 13, 2019.

SELECT BIBLIOGRAPHY

Baker, Al. "When Opioid Addicts Find an Ally in Blue," *The New York Times*, June 12, 2017, https://www.nytimes.com/2017/06/12/nyregion/when-opioid-addicts-find-an-ally-in-blue.html?searchResultPosition=1

CDC: Understanding the Epidemic, https://www.cdc.gov/drugoverdose/epidemic/index.html

Hakim, Danny, Roni Caryn Rabin, and William K. Rashbaum, "Lawsuits Lay Bare Sackler Family's Role in Opioid Crisis," *The New York Times*, April 1, 2019, https://www.nytimes.com/2019/04/01/health/sacklers-oxycontin-lawsuits.html

The Joint Commission, "Pain Management Standards—Hospital," January 1, 2018, https://www.jointcommission.org/topics/pain_management_standards_hospital.aspx

Joseph, Elizabeth, "Purdue Pharmacy Files for Bankruptcy Following Proposed Agreement to Settle Opioid Lawsuits," CNN.com, September 16, 2019, https://www.cnn.com/2019/09/16/us/purdue-pharma-bankruptcy-filing/index.html

Jones, Mark R., Omar Viswanath, Jacquelin Peck, Alan D. Kaye, Jatinder S. Gill, and Thomas T. Simopoulos, "A Brief History of the Opioid Epidemic and Strategies for Pain Medicine," NCBI, June 2018, https://www.ncbi.nlm.nih.gov/pmc/articles/PMC5993682/

Katz, Josh, "Short Answers to Hard Questions About the Opioid Crisis." *The New York Times*, August 10, 2017, https://www.nytimes.com/interactive/2017/08/03/upshot/opioid-drug-overdose-epidemic.html

Katz, Josh, and Margot Sanger-Katz, "'The Numbers Are So Staggering.' Overdose Deaths Set a Record Last Year," *The New York Times*, November 29, 2018, https://www.nytimes.com/interactive/2018/11/29/upshot/fentanyl-drug-overdose-deaths.html

Alan Mozes, "Opioid Prescriptions Tied to Perks for Doctors," WebMD, May 14, 2018, https://www.webmd.com/mental-health/addiction/news/20180514/opioid-prescriptions-tied-to-perks-for-doctors#1

Poison Control: History of the Opioid Epidemic, https://www.poison.org/articles/opioid-epidemic-history-and-prescribing-patterns-182

Quinones, Sam, "Physicians Get Addicted Too," *The Atlantic*, May 2019, https://www.theatlantic.com/magazine/archive/2019/05/opioid-epidemic-west-virginia-doctor/586036/

The Recovery Village, "The History and Tracking of Fentanyl," April 26, 2019, https://www.therecoveryvillage.com/fentanyl-addiction/where-does-fentanyl-come-from/#gref

Ryan, Benjamin, "Dying to Entertain Us: Celebrities Keep ODing on Opioids and No One Cares," *Village Voice*, July 17, 2018,https://www.villagevoice.com/2018/07/17/dying-to-entertain-us-why-celebrities-keep-dying-of-opioids/

Safe Roads: MOTOR VEHICLE TRAFFIC FATALITIES & FATALITY RATE: 1899–2003, http://www.saferoads.org/federal/2004/TrafficFatalities1899-2003.pdfs

Sanger-Katz, Margot, and Thomas Kaplan, "Congress Is Writing Lots of Opioid Bills. But Which Ones Will Actually Help?" *The New York Times*, June 20, 2018, https://www.nytimes.com/2018/06/20/upshot/congress-is-writing-lots-of-opioid-bills-but-which-ones-will-actually-help.html

Seelye, Katharine Q., "In Heroin Crisis, White Families Seek Gentler War on Drugs." *The New York Times*, October 30, 2015, https://www.nytimes.com/2015/10/31/us/heroin-war-on-drugs-parents.html?searchResultPosition=1

All internet sites accessed September 16, 2019.

About the Author

Eric Braun is an award-winning writer and editor specializing in academic and social-emotional topics. He lives in Minneapolis. Learn more at heyericbraun.com.

INDEX